Introduction

A picture of Hungarian protesters on October 25, 1956

For a considerable length of time, a significant part of the West looked on with scorn as the Bolsheviks took power in Russia and made and solidified the Soviet Union. As awful as Vladimir Lenin appeared to be in the mid twentieth century, Joseph Stalin was such a lot of more regrettable that Churchill later commented of Lenin, "Their most noticeably terrible incident was his introduction to the world... their next most exceedingly awful his passing." Before World War II, Stalin merged his situation by regularly cleansing party pioneers (most broadly Leon Trotsky) and Red Army pioneers, executing countless individuals in any event. Furthermore in one of history's most noteworthy common cases of the possibility that the foe of my adversary is my companion, Stalin's Soviet Union aligned with Britain and the United States to overcome Hitler in Europe during World War II.

Stalin had managed with an iron clench hand for almost 30 years before his passing in 1953, which could conceivably have been murder, similarly as Stalin was getting ready to lead another cleanse. With his passing, Soviet strongman and long-term Stalinist Nikita Khrushchev (1894-1971), who had figured out how to remain a stride in front of Stalin's cleanses if by some stroke of good luck since he took an interest in them, turned into the Soviet premier.

A scarcely known figure outside of the Eastern coalition, Khrushchev was disparaged as a bozo by one Western ambassador and derided for his actual appearance by others, yet any Western expectations that he would demonstrate a more propitiatory figure than Stalin were immediately snuffed out as the firm stance Khrushchev accepted angry positions. Every step of the way, Khrushchev took the strategy of conflict over pacification. An adherent to a definitive predominance of the Soviet framework, Khrushchev needed to situate the Soviet Union as a player on the world stage, an equivalent toward the Western Allies. His view was summed up in something said to Western representatives at the Polish Embassy in Moscow: "We will cover you."

Khrushchev didn't have all the earmarks of being participating in metaphor either, on the grounds that the assertion came as Soviet powers were pounding an uprising in Hungary that prompted the passings of almost 4,000 Hungarians.

After D-Day had everything except fixed the Allied triumph, Stalin's Red Army turned out to be more forceful in retaking land once held by Germany.
oncerned over the steadily augmenting Soviet guide, Churchill met with Stalin in October 1944 (Roosevelt was at this point too delicate to even think about going along with them) and, while surrendering Rumania and Bulgaria to the Soviets, demanded that Yugoslavia and Hungary be divided between the partners. The staying point at the time appeared to be Poland. Stalin requested that the extremely hostile to socialist Polish government someplace far off, banished in shame be toppled for a one more thoughtful to his regime.
Churchill, then again, felt an awareness of others' expectations to the public authority as it remained, since they were hanging out in London. Notwithstanding, he shrewdly consented to table the subject until the finish of the conflict was obviously in sight.

As it ended up, nonetheless, the Soviets would not surrender any of the region the Red Army took while pushing the Wehrmacht back to Berlin in the last option phases of World War II, guaranteeing that the Iron Curtain would wrap quite a bit of Central and Eastern Europe. In a matter of moments by any means, a large portion of these nations were changed into tyrant, socialist, one-party states, and rivals were banished or imprisoned.

Nations like Poland, Hungary, East Germany, Yugoslavia, Romania, and Czechoslovakia would sit among a coalition of socialist states partnered to the Soviet Union, and they would not rise out of this political circumstance for another 40 years.

In 1955, Moscow had united every one of the satellites as a component of the Warsaw Pact, an aggregate security association to challenge the North

Atlantic Treaty Organization (NATO), which had been established in 1949 by the United States and Western European partners. Regardless, the mid-1950s were turbulent for the Soviet Bloc. A few nations saw Stalin's demise and the clear course adjustment, even the conditioning of strategy under Khrushchev, as a chance to seek after a reformist way. In East Germany, Poland, and Hungary, showings against the socialist systems initiated vulnerability, and Hungarian pioneers endeavored to join the protestors and orientate themselves towards the West, prompting an infamous Soviet invasion.

nly infrequently did the people groups of the alleged Eastern Bloc endeavor to break liberated from the state of affairs, or possibly register their disappointment. These mass shows and uprisings go about as markers of the Cold War, incorporating 1953 in East Berlin, 1968 in Czechoslovakia, 1980–81 in Poland, and, obviously, 1989 in East Germany, Czechoslovakia and Romania. The fall of the Berlin Wall is probable the most well known, however the uprising with the best effect on the main part of the Cold War occurred in Hungary in 1956, when protestors rampaged to request independence from oppression and a more noteworthy say in their own destiny.

When the Hungarians ascended against the state of affairs in October 1956, they were met with a fierce reaction from Moscow. The historical backdrop of Hungary is one of a country that accomplished practically consistent development and compression, alongside influxes of independence and mastery. It is this feeling of history that assumed such a prevailing part in 1956 and why the concealment of the Hungarian Revolution has such a burning spot in the public awareness. Most importantly, 1956 achieved a feeling of powerlessness that Hungary had minimal opportunity to step a way of public self-assurance, as the danger of Soviet military intercession loomed over the country.

obviously, that was the Soviets' aim from the beginning. By pounding the Hungarian Uprising, the Soviets hosed the expectations of individuals of Central and Eastern Europe that they could possibly seek after a more free disapproved of way. The one special case for this standard would be Tito's Yugoslavia.

he Soviet Invasion of Hungary in 1956: The History and Legacy of the Hungarian Uprising and the Military Operations That Put It Down checks out the occasions that achieved the most well known defiance to Soviet authority during the Cold War. Alongside pictures of notable individuals and

places, you will find out with regards to the Soviet intrusion of Hungary like never before.

The War for Hungary

Hungary was a little country by 1956, struck by bigger powers toward each path, however guests to Budapest can take a gander at the great

magnificence of the city's structures, set on the banks of the superb
Danube River, and understand this was not generally the situation.
Hungary had flourished before World War I as a component of the
Habsburg double government working out of Vienna and Budapest, and it
was solely after that terrible conflict that Hungary was decreased to a
lessened status.

Religion was one more significant piece of Hungary's turn of events. In
the ninth century, the terrains presently considered Hungary were attacked
by the Magyars, a gathering of clans that combine into the Hungarian
public. The Magyars changed over to Christianity around 100 years after
the fact, yet their situation in the focal point of Europe allowed them to stay
uncovered to attack and mastery from all sides.
Hungary, as the domain became known, was battled about
perpetually for quite a long time, from both the East and the West.

he vital partitioning line, notwithstanding, happened when the Ottoman
Empire came into contact with the Habsburgs in the sixteenth century. For
the Hungarians, they were on the bleeding edges of a heavenly conflict
among Christendom and the Muslim "trespassers" from the East, yet
ultimately the Habsburgs took control
of Hungary and the nation entered a time of more noteworthy success. As
far as legislative issues and worldwide relations, Hungary would look to
amplify its self-assurance at each chance, either through coalitions or by
opposing more prominent powers.

A significant crossroads in Hungary's set of experiences came in 1867.
Hungarians were discontent with Habsburg control, and by this point the
lengthy Habsburg regal family had controlled a lot of Europe for quite a
long time, radiating from the supreme capital in Vienna. Various uprisings
had occurred, enough to truly stress the Austrian Habsburgs, and the
1860s were a novel time of Austrian shortcoming after the domain had a
lost area to an assembled Italy and accordingly to Prussia. Austria would
then lose its superior spot in the German-talking world to the recently
bound together German Empire after Prussia joined Germany during the
Franco-Prussian War.

Rebellions in different pieces of the Habsburg Empire, especially in
Slav terrains, further weakend Austrian power, and Vienna was so
concerned by

Hungarian separatists that it made an astounding concession in 1867, consenting to impart power inside its realm to Hungary, in the purported Austro-Hungarian Compromise. The domain then, at that point, became known as the Austro-Hungarian Empire.

With that, Hungary entered one of its best, stable, and prosperous authentic stages. Budapest turned into the capital of a worldwide, multiethnic domain with clout inside Europe and then some. Monetarily, Hungary surpassed the greater part of its adversaries in the very nearly 50 years of its magnificent standard and gained ground mechanically and financially, including urbanization.

For the non-Hungarian people groups living inside the realm, be that as it may, the Austro-Hungarian period was one of dissatisfaction. The late nineteenth century achieved the ascent of patriotism, and a large number of the other Slav countries needed their own states, including the Czechs, Slovaks, and Croats to name yet a few.
Furthermore, the Hungarians managed in a more draconian manner than their Austrian accomplices as Budapest looked to grow its impact and "Magyarize" the non-Hungarians subject to their authority. This was a reason for extraordinary discontent to any semblance of the Slovaks, who started to shake for more noteworthy autonomy.

Naturally, the breakdown of the domain in 1918 demonstrated calamitous for Hungarian power, impact, and success, notwithstanding the reality the contention had barely anything to do with Hungary itself. The fight that catalyzed the First World War was among Austria and Serbia, coming after a Serb patriot, Gavrilo Princip, killed the successor to the Austrian lofty position, Archduke Franz Ferdinand. At the incredible power level, it was the Triple Entente of France, Britain, and Russia that went against Austria and Germany. Each bigger domain was careful about the apparent development of the others, and Hungary was basically a commentary in the more extensive showdown between the two alliances.

Despite endeavors to control Vienna and work strategically to keep up with harmony, Hungary together left upon the conflict and assisted with the assault on Serbia in August 1914, regardless of whether plainly Vienna was the senior accomplice. In certain regards, it was actually the sort of social closed-mindedness showed by the Hungarian experts long before 1914 that so angered the minorities in the domain and made separatists ascend. Worried that Vienna should add-on more land in the

Balkans as a conflict point, Hungary, including Prime Minister Count István Tisza, contended against battle in 1914, not

needing more "furious Slavs" in its territory.[1] Nonetheless, the Austrians needed to show the Serbs something new and forestall further strain inside the empire.

Tisza

Hungary endured during the conflict, demonstrating helpless against assaults from each possible bearing, and throughout the span of the conflict the Hungarians lost countless soldiers during the contention and an innumerable number of regular citizens, even as the Austro-Hungarian Empire had altogether less conflict points than different belligerents. Vienna needed to check Serb dissidence inside Bosnia-Hercegovina and to harden its traction on the Balkan Peninsula, basically meaning Austria only intended to stand up against its apparent international decrease over the past decades.

As plainly it was going to lose the contention, spirit plummeted among the populace, while others, strikingly dissidents, communists, and patriots, saw their chance to overpower the current request. An illustration of the tumult that grasped Hungary toward the finish of the conflict was the death on October 31, 1918 of pre-war Prime Minister Count István Tisza, when disappointed officers and miscreants broke into his home.

An autonomous Czechoslovakia was declared, upheld by the Entente Powers. The Slovak part of the new state had been administered, fairly miserably, by Budapest during its supreme rule. One more global league, Yugoslavia, was declared in 1918, comprised of Serbia and Montenegro in addition to domain which had recently had a place with the Austria-Hungary and Ottoman Empires, in Croatia, Bosnia Hercegovina, Macedonia and Slovenia. These progressions were formailized at Versailles.
Meanwhile, different states peered toward parts of Hungary, for example, the resuscitated Poland and an expansionist Romania.

When Russia changed because of the Bolshevik Revolution in 1917 and looked for a peace negotiation in the blink of an eye subsequently, it created the impression that Serbia had lost its indispensable advocate, however the conflict finished the next year with British, Italian, and French soldiers at last crushing the Germans, Austro-Hungarians, and Ottomans. Those Balkan nations that had conformed to the Allied powers would absolutely help when the post-war international reduced was settled at Versailles.

With the old domains shredded before the finish of the conflict, and with Russia debilitated by its upheaval, British and French power currently overwhelmed in the Balkans. Both had gigantic abroad realms of their own and were quick to grow their impact in the more extensive locale, from the Balkans to the Middle East and North Africa. Vitally for the account of Austria and Hungary, Britain
and France both inclined toward Serbia.[2] Some essayists have placed this with regards to the heartfelt patriots that came to noticeable quality in the nineteenth century, in light of on freeing the Greeks (Philhellenism) from the Ottoman Empire and afterward other Christian public developments in the area. To be sure, London was home to various banished patriot developments. Nonetheless, the almost certain justification behind the British and French help was that the Serbs made up

the biggest unforeseen in the West Balkan region. Subsequently, support for Serbia might have offered the bigger abilities their best any desire for solidness, and this transformed into help for a Serb-drove Slavic state.

One of the images of the period, Emperor Franz Josef, kicked the bucket in 1916, supplanted by the 29-year-old Karl I. The domain would endure yet two years without its longstanding nonentities, and when the Habsburgs ceded in October 1918, it all the while broke the joining among Austria and Hungary.

The Treaty of Versailles was a sledge hit to the Central Powers. The triumphant nations generally felt distressed and needed conflict repayments and a victor's equity, if not vengeance, yet the predominant power at the 1919 Versailles harmony gathering was President Woodrow Wilson and the United States.
Wilson vowed to advocate public self-assurance for unrepresented people groups, which would strip Hungary of notoriety, and when the harmony was reached, Hungary kept just 28% (36,000 square kilometers) of its territory.

he Treaty of Versailles, endorsed in June 1919, contracted Hungary from all sides,[3] and these progressions were additionally settled in by the Treaty of Saint-Germain and, most fundamentally, the Treaty of Trianon. The Treaty of Trianon was endorsed in Versailles on June 4, 1920 among Hungary and the
successful powers, very nearly one year after the significant post-war understanding. In certain regards, Hungary was the country most cruelly managed after the conflict, in light of the fact that as well as paying restitutions and having its military restricted, Hungary surrendered domain to Romania, Austria, Czechoslovakia, and Yugoslavia.

Although Budapest held out some expectation that the United States may take a gentler line with it in shame, the Americans marked the Treaty of Trianon close by different victors. The settlement was one of the first to be directed by the recently shaped League of Nations, and the new boundaries have remained basically unaltered for current Hungary from that point forward. The conflict stripped Hungary of its admittance to the ocean, and most agonizingly, it was assessed that 2 million ethnic Hungarians currently lived outside the Hungarian state. This was exceptionally questionable, especially when it came to surrendering area to Romania, especially in Transylvania where north of 1,000,000 Magyars lived.

Post-War Socialism

Hungary proclaimed a majority rule republic soon after the conflict reached a conclusion, yet it would be fleeting prior to being supplanted by the Kingdom of Hungary, which appeared after the Treaty of Trianon. As that

recommends, Hungary's concerns were aggravated by political tumult inside the state toward the finish of World War I. A few communist insurgencies were holding Europe, remembering for parts of Germany and, most broadly, in Russia. Two transformations in 1917 had removed Tsar Nicholas II and permitted Vladimir Lenin's Bolsheviks to hold onto power in a socialist overthrow. Another express, the Soviet Union, was shaped, just to slip into common conflict until the mid 1920s. In international terms, this implied that Russia had little say in the Versailles cycle and the consequence of the First World War. In philosophical terms, the possibility of communist upheaval charmed numerous across the landmass, remembering for Hungary.

**Len
in**

It is some of the time affirmed that the socialist system that came to
control after the Second World War in Hungary was exclusively forced
from Moscow and that 1956 was a dismissal of this philosophy. The truth,
in any case, was less direct. Revolutionary left-wing legislative issues did
indeed have some hang on the Hungarian populace, a long time before the
Cold War, as clarified by the 1919 "Soviet" system of Béla Kun. An
unrest had occurred in Hungary toward the finish of 1918, drove by Count
Mihály Károlyi and maybe best depicted as friendly fair in nature. The
Károlyi system had been key in compelling the break with Austria,

however this temporary government was constrained from power in
March 1919 during a subsequent upset, this time drove by socialists. The
new government, by that mid year, declared itself as the Hungarian Soviet
Republic, continuing in the strides of Soviet Russia. It was driven by
President
ándor Garbai and, all the more altogether, Foreign Minister Béla Kun.[4]
Lenin himself was supposed to be in direct contact with Kun.

Kun

During its couple of months in power, this system regulated one of the
most fierce periods in the nation's set of experiences. Béla Kun's socialist
local armies carried out a ruthless cleanse of every one of those went
against to the new system, even the Social Democrats, and by utilizing
the Soviet style, little laborers' portrayals were set up while the anciens

system was taken out. Property and agrarian land were nationalized, and free instructive projects were established.

Budapest was the bedrock of communist help, however the remainder of the country outside the significant urban areas stayed went against to the system. With regards to other progressive socialist systems, state armies, for example, the infamous "Lenin

Boys" were conveyed into the nation to observe those went against to the system, and in what became known as the "Red Terror," mass executions of hundreds were completed in specially appointed councils, which increased when the Social Democrats fruitlessly endeavored to retake power in June. Mihály Károlyi, in the mean time, escaped someplace far off, banished in shame in France, and dread, viciousness, and concealment would torment Hungary in the coming many years, including past the 1956 uprising.

hile the homegrown plan (in case one can consider it that) of the socialists was turbulent, the outside arrangements demonstrated similarly as confounded and rough. Béla Kun and his companions might have been logically internationalist socialists, however when confronted with outside impedance, they showed a solid feeling of nationalism. In May 1919, the Entente Powers needed the Hungarian system to consent to regional concessions, however this was met with shock by the Hungarians' purported Red Army, who opposed the difference in borders with the Slovaks and afterward the Romanians. Albeit the Hungarians had some tactical achievement, it was clear they were probably not going to accomplish extreme triumph against the powers consolidated against them, and when Kun's soldiers pulled back from Slovakia and afterward Romania subsequent to having been guaranteed by the French that the Romanians would likewise withdraw, the socialist government lost the help of the military. Truth be told, the Romanians didn't withdraw and utilized the trickiness without limit. Toward the finish of July 1919, the socialist system imploded and key figures, for example, Béla Kun went far away, banished for good. The Romanians, in the mean time, walked on Budapest and had involved the capital by early August. It was one more grave shock to Hungary's public regard. On schedule, Miklós Horthy would arise in 1919, introducing himself as beneficiary of the Hungarian lofty position, and right after Horthy taking power, the left would be cleansed. Responses occurred for very nearly two years, prompting an expected 1,000 dead and a lot more imprisoned.

**Hor
thy**

Hungary was quite welcome to Versailles in 1919, however this was withdrawn because of the unsteadiness inside the country, then, at that point, in the holds of the Garbai-Kun system and reestablished struggle with Romania. Hungary was welcomed again in November 1919 once Horthy was in office, yet by then, at that point, the greater part of the significant issues had been chosen when the Hungarian assignment showed up. Despite the fact that Russia had battled on a similar side as the Entente during the First

World War, relations had in practically no time soured after the 1917 transformation and the replacement socialist system's withdrawal from the Eastern Front, basically giving Germany victory.[5] As the Russian Civil War worked out over the
following years, France and Britain supported the "white" hostile to communist
powers. Hence, when comparable progressive occasions gave off an impression of being working out in Hungary, the Entente demonstrated fast to back traditionalist powers, for this situation Horthy's soldiers. However, the victors at Versailles were not ready to give Hungary further concessions in the harmony arrangements. The Entente needed the Austro-Hungarian Empire destroyed and individual countries addressed in cautious states. This was at last never conceivable because of the blended identities of generally Central and Eastern European countries.
Even the enormously decreased Hungary was not even close to homogeneous. They included critical quantities of ethnic Romanians, Ruthenians and Germans, and albeit overwhelmingly Christian, additionally included numerous Jews.

Although the moderators evidently needed to remember separate ethnicities for the post-war European states (and surprisingly offer plebiscites to the absolute most challenged regions), the Transylvania locale was one which got just inadequate consideration. Romania had supported its wagers during the conflict, just entering the contention in 1916 on the Entente. The Romanian armed force, nonetheless, was crushed by the Central Powers and later involved. Having been compelled to sign an embarrassing cease-fire in 1918, the nation was given a relief when Germany was beaten on the Western Front.

At that point, it seems that Bucharest was anxious to wipe away the humiliation of defeat on the battlefield with a concerted campaign diplomatically.[6] In 1919, Romanian troops attacked a weakened Hungary to press home its territorial claims. The Entente powers, perhaps surprisingly, rewarded Romania's tactics by granting it an astonishing amount of territory in Transylvania. The Hungarian moderators railed harshly against the proposed changes whenever they had sat down at Versailles, yet it was without any result. Albeit public self-assurance gave off an impression of being the thing to get done, the standard was overlooked for this situation, as a great many Hungarians would be cut off from the remainder of Hungary.

Hungary marked the Treaty of Trianon eventually, however for Hungarian patriots, the post-war arrangements addressed an attack that pointlessly reduced their country without support. The post-war border changes would accumulate complaints that could be used by new political powers during the 1930s, when the following mainland emergency emerged.

World War II

The predominant player in Hungarian governmental issues from World War I until the finish of World War II was Admiral Miklós Horthy. Naturally introduced to a privileged family, Horthy had fabricated a profession in the Hungarian Navy, ascending to the position of Rear Admiral, albeit this was to some degree amusing after the conflict since Hungary was left without admittance to the ocean. After the downfall of the socialist Garbai-Kun system in mid-1919, Horthy arose as the head of the patriots who dealt with Budapest. Horthy was not straightforwardly up to speed in the "White Terror" that followed, yet he has all things considered been
tacitly implicated by historians.[7]

Horthy was a moderate and of the right, and along these lines totally adequate likewise to the Entente powers who were at this point scared of the socialist unrest overwhelming the mainland. He was "welcomed" to sit as head of state by the Hungarian parliament, as official. This was likewise like other Eastern European expresses that were then returning to monarchical standard in the interwar period, like Romania and Yugoslavia.

The Hungarian government, close by Horthy, looked to settle the nation's messed up economy during the 1920s. This it did with moderate accomplishment under the aegis of Prime Minister István Bethlen (1921–31), until the 1929 Wall Street Crash and resulting Great Depression made major issues for the Hungarian economy.

**Bethle
n**

The essential political worry of the decade, notwithstanding, was the apparent treachery of the Treaty of Trianon, which figured out how to join Hungarians of every political tendency. The country's chiefs looked for unions with different states endeavoring to switch a portion of these changes, and Hungary likewise joined the League of Nations. Most prominently, Hungary marked a Treaty of Friendship with Benito Mussolini's Italy in 1927.

Hungary's hazardous contact with the mainland's fundamentalists proceeded into the 1930s. After some dependability in the earlier decade, the moves executed by Horthy would finish in more disaster for Hungarians, and when it remerged during the 1940s, it was indeed constrained by communists.

Following the move towards Mussolini's Italy, Hungary was stood up to by other fundamentalist developments in its neighborhood during the 1930s, especially as financial emergencies set in. Budapest's reaction was to basically embrace, instead of restricting, the extremist wave. This appeared to work for some time, until occasions plummeted into one more mainland war.

Fascism became out a specific variation of outrageous patriotism, combined with social cooperation and nativism, and these were available somewhat in Hungary during the 1930s. Patriotism was at that point unequivocally inserted in the country before the First World War and cemented during the 1920s, energized by the complaints of Trianon. In the Central and Eastern European area, extreme right patriot and fundamentalist developments filled in Bulgaria, Romania, Slovakia, and Yugoslavia, and in Hungary it became pervasive when Horthy eliminated Bethlen as Prime Minister in 1931 and supplanted him (after a short intermission with Gyula Károlyi in office) with the proto-extremist Gyula Gömbös. In power until 1936, Gömbös had recently been viewed as hostile to Semitic and addressed the shift to one side in Hungary during the period. Truth be told, subterranean insect Semitism had been an issue in Hungary for quite a while, and during the White Terror, hostile to socialism feeling was frequently conflated with hostile to Semitism, prompting savagery against Jews. Rough enemy of semitism would return during the 1930s and arrive at a terrible crescendo during the Second World War.

**Göm
bös**

Prime Minister Gömbös looked for, not without reason, to expand exchange joins with Italy and Germany as a method for invigorating the Hungarian economy. Gömbös had additionally been given confirmations by the fundamentalist nations that they would uphold Hungary's endeavors to switch Trianon. This definitely implied Hungary would be defenseless against the international affairs of the period, and by the mid-1930s, the mainland was split between just powers and fundamentalist powers. The Spanish Civil War, beginning in 1936, was proof of this, as well as the float of many nations' interior legislative issues towards the extremes.[8] Hungary was indeed trapped in a bigger showdown, and by and by the Hungarians would wind up on the losing side.

Kálmán Darányi took over as Hungarian Prime Minister in 1936 and imparted a few attributes to Horthy. Albeit not an out and out fundamentalist, he in any case had a few feelings, was conservative, and basically a dictator. Darányi fixed the public authority's political hold at home while seeking after outside strategies amicable to Mussolini's Italy and Hitler's Germany. By the by, Darányi went under expanding pressure locally from the Arrow Cross Party, framed in 1935 by Ferenc Szálasi, which looked for not exclusively to upset the Trianon settlement yet did as such in the style of other European fundamentalist gatherings. The party was transparently against Semitic and repeated Hitler's cases of a "Jewish-Bolshevist trick." Arrow Cross didn't get genuine clout, in any case, until the Second World War.

Dará
nyi

One of the reasons Hungary's lawmakers played a particularly hazardous game with the extremist powers during the 1930s was that they accepted that this was the most obvious opportunity for them to recover their pre-Trianon region. Horthy visited Hitler in Germany requesting help with this undertaking, while Hitler needed help for his proposed attack of Czechoslovakia. In September 1938 at the Munich Conference, Hitler got consent to add-on the

German-talking part of Czechoslovakia, the alleged Sudetenland,[9] and Horthy's help for that addition seemed to have delivered profits as Hungary involved a space of Southeast Czechoslovakia containing ethnic

Hungarians without further ado afterwards.

As Germany trampled the Versailles settlement, Hungary gained a greater amount of the land it had lost. In 1939 it was "in truth" Carpathian Ruthenia (today for the most part situated in Ukraine), and in 1940 it got Transylvania from Romania in the purported "Vienna Awards." By then the Second World War had begun, and despite the fact that Horthy could feel fulfilled he had somewhat upset the much-detested Treaty of Trianon, he had favored Nazi Germany and would before long face the consolidated fury of the Allies, incorporating the Soviet Union.

n the last part of the 1930s, the Hungarian ploy seemed to have paid off. Horthy had regulated (under the oversight of Hitler) the reacquisition of terrains in Czechoslovakia and Romania, and in mid 1939 Pál Teleki became state head for the subsequent time. Both Teleki and Horthy endeavored to protect Hungary from the conflict, what began in September 1939, and keeping in mind that this worked in the beginning stage of the contention, this way turned out to be always unstable as time continued. At first, Hungary had rejected German solicitations to utilize their nation as a method for travel, yet unavoidably the Hungarians would be hauled into the worldwide conflict.

In 1940-41, Southern and Eastern Europe were sucked into the conflict as the Nazis tried to grow their organization of partners by making manages Romania and proto-extremists in Croatia.[10] In so doing, borders were redrawn, and Hitler could utilize the complaints numerous in the district actually held onto from Versailles. This was all important for the more extensive procedure to kill and conquer
land in the east, especially in the Soviet Union. The Nazis saw the Slavic people groups as subhuman, and Hitler's longstanding abhorrence to Bolshevism was notable. The Soviet Union's region additionally had significant ramifications for the conflict exertion since it had an immense archive of unrefined substances and energy.

For Hungary, this implied that the fundamentalists needed to ask for help they had allowed Budapest over the earlier years. In 1940, it had to join the Axis and was basically made docile to Germany, even as it needed to manage the tactical powers contradicting the Nazis in the theater. Hungary submitted troops to Axis military missions in both the Soviet Union and Yugoslavia.

The tide of the conflict turned in 1942, especially at Stalingrad, where numerous Hungarians lost their lives. After a progression of fights across

the front, the Soviet Red Army began to move back German powers, guaranteeing the eventual
rout of the Nazis.

In Hungary, the veteran moderate Miklós Kállay was named state head, and he expanded the political persecution of Jews and different minorities. For Hitler, however, this Naziesque oppression was sufficiently not, and he associated Kállay and Horthy with trying to remove themselves from the Axis and join the Allies. Subsequently, in 1944, the Germans attacked and involved Hungary, bringing the merciless idea of the contention to the country.

vents moved rapidly in Hungary in 1944–45, establishing the vibe for the quick consequence and the advancement of its post-war socialist system. After the Nazis attacked in March 1944, another top state leader was selected, the extremist Döme Sztójay, who then, at that point, legitimized the Arrow Cross Party but at the same time was managed by a Nazi governor.

Sztój
ay

If the conditions had been severe for Hungarian Jews before the Nazi intrusion, their circumstance crumbled quickly from there on. More than 430,000 Jews were ousted to Nazi concentration camps like Auschwitz, and comparable treatment was distributed to the nation's Roma, 28,000 of whom were killed. Bolt Cross volunteer armies were particularly ensnared

as far as concerns them in the
Holocaust in Hungary.[11]

In October 1944, the Soviet Red Army crossed into Hungarian domain and started the fight to push the Nazis out of the country. The Hungarian government, for example, it existed, was then parted into groups, with an extremist drove Government of National Unity. Ferenc Szálasi, of the Arrow Cross, turned into this present government's chief and sped up the abhorrences of the Holocaust.

The battling went on until April 1945, and the most eminent fight was the Battle of Budapest, which kept going from December 1944-February 1945, during which 76,000 regular folks were killed. By then, at that point, Regent Miklós Horthy was frantic to sign a peace negotiation and join the Allies, however he had to venture down and was taken prisoner by the Nazis.

When the Allies' significant chiefs met at Yalta in mid 1945, Stalin advised the others about Soviet advancement in Europe. The plan for the principal day's conversation comprised for the most part of military issues. The Soviets gave the Western Allies the primary nitty gritty instructions on the Eastern front circumstance and their prompt hostile plans. General of the Army Aleksei Antonov, talking through Stalin's own translator Vladimir Pavlov, given the report. He laid out the amazing Soviet winter hostile that drove synchronous pushes through Poland, Hungary, and East Prussia, bewildering the Westerners with the degree and achievement of the Soviet advance.

Roosevelt, showing that his psyche stayed dynamic under the veil of ailment that occasionally caused him to show up practically mental, posed a shockingly infiltrating inquiry. He intruded on Antonov, finding out if the Russians had changed over the railroads in Eastern Europe from European check to the more extensive Soviet measure to raise their provisions. The inquiry addressed more than inactive interest, since, in such a case that the Soviets had revamped the railroads to coordinate with their own measure, then, at that point, long-lasting occupation appeared to be almost certain. Antonov, put a spotlight on, answered that the Soviets had to be sure supplanted the European measure rail route with their own. This inferred affirmation of victory, rather than freedom, drew one more clever comment from the American president: "As our militaries are presently moving toward one another in Germany it was significant that the staffs ought to talk about this issue so that there would be a clear spot in Germany where the various checks would meet."

The result of the Yalta Conference remains exceptionally questionable in understandings of World War II. Some recognition the Western Allies for winning

more than they may somehow have through adept arrangement with the forceful Soviet state. Others denounce Roosevelt as either a guileless numb-skull or even a kind of quisling, neglecting to counter Stalin's requests and along these lines leaving Eastern Europe to its destiny as the footrest of the persistent Stalinist empire.

indeed, however proof can be brushed from the records to help numerous perspectives, the most conceivable clarification stays that the Yalta Conference demonstrated to a great extent worthless generally on the grounds that little space for conversation existed. Stalin previously held a most the area his nation would hold dominance over until the disintegration of the Soviet Union. With such a solid position – fundamentally unassailable, with the Red Army developed anew by enormous Lend-Lease help and homegrown creation, and sharpened to a generally proficient power – the Soviet chief had no justifiable excuse to yield an inch on Poland or the remainder of Eastern Europe, and indeed he didn't. Roosevelt and Churchill just had no influence at all to constrain Stalin to reestablish the opportunity of his new customer states. They could offer minimal the Soviets didn't as of now have, and with the Third Reich still effectively at war, they couldn't hazard a full break with Stalin that may (as they accepted) cause the two despots to join once more. Shy of pronouncing battle on the Soviet Union and overcoming it in a broad fight, the American and British heads of state had no choices to incite Stalin's compliance.

ne other burden hampered the Western Allies' dealings. Their records incidentally uncovered them, notwithstanding their political discernment, to be fundamentally legitimate men. They would in general need to trust the best of Stalin and the Soviets, fully trusting tokens of benevolence. Both, especially Roosevelt, neglected indications of Soviet antagonism, accepting Stalin to be a "great individual" at base, one who preferred them and needed to arrive at a commonly advantageous agreement. While recollecting practicality and showing expertise and surprisingly intermittent trickery working inside their own vote based frameworks, they actually showed obviously that they came from a generally cultivated political environment. They showed similarly open and confiding in characters, and a reflexive suspicion that their Soviet partner would, somewhat in any event, "follow the rules." Both men had limits they would not pass.

Stalin, the result of a dangerous upset and a significantly more lethal autocracy who made due and ruled through injustice, ruthlessness, and fear among the savage, destructive men including the Soviet power structure,

used a guile his all the more candid Western partners demonstrated unprepared to coordinate. The Soviet despot had administered a state established on mass executions, torment, jail camps, death, designed starvation, and the absolute predominance of the state over each aspect of public and private life. He perceived no restrictions to his activities; he expected to win, and he applied all his significant crafty to accomplishing this goal.

Furthermore, he detested the two men he managed venomously, regardless of his outward demonstration of agreeableness. One of his tirades to Yugoslav socialist pioneer Milovan Djilas in 1944 uncovered his actual abhorring of Roosevelt and Churchill as the personified delegates of an entrepreneur framework he completely defamed and wished to obliterate: "Maybe you imagine that since we are the partners of the English we have   forgotten what their identity is [...] And Churchill?
hurchill is the sort who, assuming you don't watch him, will slip a kopeck out of your pocket. Indeed, a kopeck out of your pocket! By God, a kopeck out of your pocket! What's more Roosevelt? Roosevelt isn't care for that. He plunges in his grasp just for greater coins. Yet, Churchill? Churchill—in any event, for a kopeck."

Either way, while Yalta addressed a general disappointment for Roosevelt and Churchill on most matters, the power of situation couldn't make it in any case. Stalin held the strategic position on the vast majority of the issues being talked about and, obviously, arose with the greater part of the domains and concessions he needed, since he previously delighted possessing them.

Churchill, Roosevelt, and Stalin at the Yalta Conference

various harmony gatherings were met during and after the conflict, most broadly in Yalta and Potsdam in 1945, yet in addition in this manner in London and Paris. The early gatherings of the United Nations likewise prepared for the post-war world. For Hungary, the pivotal gathering was held in Paris once more, and like Versailles in 1919 and 1920, its initiative had to surrender an area and face further embarrassments. The extraordinary issues in Central and Eastern Europe were, generally, settled in the 1947 Paris Peace Treaty, and Hungary had to surrender the regions it had obtained as a component of its coalition with the Nazis, basically getting back to its pre-1938 lines. Subsequently, Budapest needed to return the regions it had attached in Czechoslovakia and Romania, thus called populace trades were formalized, permitting the questionable act of moving specific ethnicities into independent states. This most famously happened with the ejections of the ethnic Germans from the area to Germany itself. For Hungary's situation, the 1947 arrangement built up that of Trianon in 1920. In the interwar period, patriot Hungarian legislators could squeeze home the case for reconquering the lost terrains or accomplishing this through arrangement, yet after the Second World War this was everything except outlandish on the grounds that the lawmakers who drove the nation were agreeable to Moscow and thusly probably not going to be patriots. Besides, all the region a growing Hungary may have ached for was presently in the Eastern Bloc. This multitude of nations fell under the Soviet range of prominence and military umbrella and would proceed to shape a clear "fellowship" of socialist nations.

obviously, Hungary itself had been crushed when the conflict finished in Europe in May 1945. A huge number of Hungarian soldiers had been killed on the Eastern Front, and the nation's Jewish and Roma populaces were overpowered by the coordinated slaughter of the Holocaust.

In a similar vein, the fleeting regional increases of the last part of the 1930s and mid 1940s were ancient remnants of the past. One of the essential drivers of Hungarian arrangement between the conflicts and in the mid 1940s was the craving to keep up with some level of independence, and even boost Budapest's impact and prestige.
The occasions of the Second World War and the country's coalition with the fundamentalist nations, be that as it may, prompted the perfect inverse. The nation was pushed to the brink of collapse during the conflict, compelled to submit individuals and assets against its desires, and eventually, Hungary finished the conflict in a more regrettable situation than it had been in toward the finish of World War I. This time, rather than holding a more modest autonomous country, Hungary was involved by the Red Army.

Occupation and Stalinization

Despite the endeavors of a portion of Hungary's chiefs to separate themselves from the Axis toward the finish of the contention, the Soviets would not show tolerance. Naturally, a significant number of Hungary's most unmistakable extremists escaped the country toward the finish of the conflict, unfortunate of the potential retaliation coming from the Soviet Red Army.[12] The retribution of Stalin's soldiers would for sure be fierce – subsequent to having been assaulted by the Nazis in 1941 and enduring huge number of setbacks, the Soviet soldiers became notorious for the barbarities they released upon the populaces they involved as they beat back the fundamentalist forces.

Initially for the Hungarians, the section of the Red Army into their nation offered the chance of finishing the enduring of the conflict. In addition, there was a remaining compassion towards communism from a considerable extent of

the population, and the Soviets had some cachet since they had ended the Nazi occupation.[113]

Any help the Soviets appreciated among wraps of the Hungarian populace would disperse rapidly. Almost immediately over the span of the occupation, a huge number of Hungarians were expelled to the famous Gulag work camps in the Soviet Union, and a considerable lot of these detainees died.

elated to that, the Soviets endeavored to force their philosophy onto the people groups of Central and Eastern Europe. The Soviet military commandant in Hungary, Marshal Kliment Voroshilov, attempted to load the temporary government with socialists and afterward influence races. The Soviet-moved socialist forerunners in the November 1945 Hungarian races were Mátyás Rákosi and Ernő Gerő, yet they neglected to get the triumph for which they, and Voroshilov, were trusting, taking just 17% of the vote. The races were predominantly won by the Independent Smallholders Party, with 57% of the vote. This moderate, patriot party framed an administration, with its chief Zoltán Tildy becoming Prime Minister.

Voroshilov

Rákosi

Tildy

ildy was in power in name just, nonetheless, as the socialists orbited the passageways of force. Rákosi was brought to Moscow to get guidelines from the Stalin system concerning how his Communist Party could hold onto absolute control of the country.[14] Put basically, the Soviets were not going to surrender control of an area they had drained for during the war.

Over the following three years, the socialists would step by step fill in impact in Hungary, regardless of whether this portion of government was not coordinated by help in the country. Comparable occasions worked out across Central and Eastern Europe, remembering for East Germany and Czechoslovakia, where decisions had not inclined toward socialists, who by and by acquired the high ground in the
ensuing power struggles.[15] The process became known as Stalinization, and it was typically undergirded by an overbearing surveillance and state security apparatus that denied basic freedoms to occupied citizens. Only in Tito's Yugoslavia could the communists claim real popular legitimacy.

That said, a portion of the socialist drove changes in Hungary had some help, for example, the cancelation of the government in February 1946. Less appetizing arrangements were likewise sought after, like the ejection of by far most of Hungary's ethnic Germans between 1946–48, an expected 200,000 individuals. By August 1949, the socialist takeover of the nation was finished as the People's Republic of Hungary was announced. Hungary was currently well and really behind the "Iron Curtain" of the Cold War.

elations between the two superpowers that arose after the conflict, the United States and the Soviet Union, weakened in 1946 and 1947, and they deteriorated further past 1948. The Truman organization accepted it had been deceived by Stalin's Soviet system about its aims in Central and Eastern Europe. The Red Army was probably a transitory presence in the area, yet when plainly they were probably going to remain for the more drawn out term, the Americans reacted indignantly. This was exacerbated by the Soviet system of utilizing interior moving (basically rebellions) to place their favored socialists into places of force. A similar example of overlooking political race results and observing means for introducing a socialist chief or government repeated across the area, remembering for Hungary.

The United States attempted to forestall this with two headline policies in 1946–47.[16] The first was the Marshall Plan, which aimed to rebuild Europe's shattered economies. In return, the countries who received aid would build close relations with Washington and open their markets somewhat to
American merchandise. The deal was promptly taken up by
Western European nations. Hungary, regardless of whether it had needed to, was obstructed from looking for Marshall Plan help by Moscow, which then, at that point, set with regards to its own, considerably less alluring "Molotov Plan."[17]

part from the financial side of the superpower contention, the United States additionally set about attempting to keep nations from going "red" or tolerating socialist principle. After the activities of the Red Army in 1945 and the ensuing control of Central and Eastern Europe, the Americans were restless not to witness this once more. The experiments for their recharged approach were Greece and Turkey, the two of which were held by common war
in the late 1940s and had significant communist forces.[18] President Truman announced in 1947 that his administration would assist any

government or side in a civil conflict which resisted communism. In this instance Truman

was centered around Greece and Turkey, however this would before long effect Berlin during the 1948–49 carrier and afterward the 1950–53 Korean War. When the Hungarians ascended against socialism in 1956, in any case, the Truman Doctrine had more restricted parameters.

Following on from the Truman Doctrine, the Americans concocted a methodology that would attract its Western European partners into a security coalition. With this novel, conceivably risky rule that "an assault on one is an assault on all," the Truman organization shaped the North Atlantic Treaty Organization (NATO) in 1949. Article 5 of the NATO establishing archive set out the aggregate protection rule. This was a profoundly provocative move in Moscow's eyes, and the USSR reacted with its own aggregate security coalition, the Warsaw Pact. This was not hardened, in any case, until 1955. Before then, at that point, the Soviets expected to solidify socialism in every Central and Eastern European state.

After the November 1945 political race, the Communist Party in Hungary under Mátyás Rákosi had given a valiant effort to sabotage the public authority of the Independent Smallholders Party. Referred to by the socialist chief himself as "salami strategies," Rákosi utilized each chance to minimize the job of the senior accomplice in the public authority while at the same time taking advantage of their disorder to debilitate them. The August 1947 races were generally considered to have been manipulated, with the Independent Smallholders getting a simple 15% of the vote, down from 57% in 1945. The Communists, in any case, notwithstanding help from Moscow and after Rákosi's Machiavellian mission, could just marshal 2%, barely enough to complete first. The result allowed Rákosi his opportunity to destroy the delicate post-war democracy.

Similar moves were occurring across the district, most famously in Czechoslovakia, where the non-socialist Foreign Minister Jan Masaryk was found dead in February 1948 subsequent to having probably hopped from the window of his service. The ensuing retirement of the nation's drawn out pioneer, Edvard Beneš, allowied socialist pioneer Klement Gottwald to
become president.[19]

Events in Hungary had something of the kind of a few of its peers. Most altogether, Rákosi approached annihilating the Social Democratic Party in 1948 and 1949. The Social Democrats won 17% of the vote in November 1945 and 15% in August 1947, however Rákosi then, at that point, constrained the

Social Democrats to converge with his Communist Party in June 1948 to frame the Hungarian Working People's Party, after which he cleansed the new party of its noticeable previous anti-extremists, pushing them either out of the party or in banishment. It was a fundamentally the same as way to deal with the one taken in East Germany in the late 1940s.

The moment of truth for Hungary's development came in the summer of 1949. The pressure had built both on Hungary's communist and non-communist leaders from the Soviets, who were eager to solidify a homogenous Communist Bloc.[20] Having by now dropped all pretenses of a democracy, Rákosi joined his regional contemporaries in declaring Hungary
a clearly socialist state. Prior that year the socialist chief had, unusually, constrained each ideological group to go under the standard of the People's Front, then, at that point, proclaimed himself the pioneer and restricted all resistance groups. This then, at that point, permitted Rákosi, with the endorsement of Moscow (under the aegis of the People's Front) to pronounce a one-party state and compose another constitution in August 1949. The nation was renamed the People's Republic of Hungary, and communism was recognized as the focal overseeing reasoning. The decision Communist Party could now seek after the program of Stalinization that eventually constrained Hungarians to ascend in 1956.

After the arrangement of the Hungarian People's Republic, Rákosi approached carrying out a customary Stalinist program. With the alleged Iron Curtain presently isolating Europe, socialists in Hungary had no responsibility but to Moscow, so as anyone might expect, the socialist forerunners in Central and Eastern Europe all imitated the acts of Stalin himself. This implied the total nationalization of industry and collectivization of farming, normally with the related decrease of efficiency and yields. Afterward, the Soviets saw their customer states as expansions of the Soviet Union itself and requested that the satellites focus on specific businesses, yields, or asset extraction.

Taken together, these arrangements seriously diminished the possible limit of states, for example, Hungary.

Along with the economic mismanagement of Stalinists in Hungary, the usual purges and repression took place. Rákosi continued targeting Social Democrats who were viewed as not radical enough, but also, in true Stalinist fashion, he harassed and imprisoned rivals in the Communist Party itself.[21] This meant that during the early years of the communist regime in Hungary,

the public authority and the general public itself took a draconian and firm stance turn. The actual Soviets set up what could be compared to Hungary's mysterious police, the State Protection Authority, and they approached a mission of ruthless concealment in these early years. Rákosi's fundamental opponent in the Communist Party was Foreign Minister László Rajk, who had battled on the International Brigades in the Spanish Civil War during the 1930s and afterward in the Hungarian underground during the Second World War. Rákosi organized a show preliminary for Rajk in 1949, blaming him for being thoughtful on Stalin's left side wing adversaries, like Leon Trotsky. After a constrained admission, Rajk was indicted and afterward, amazingly, executed. It was right from the pages of the Stalinist manual, like the 1930s "Incredible Terror."

Rajk

From there, Rákosi and the State Protection Authority designated anybody with Western associations, the Church, or any connections with either the Horthy or extremist systems. It is assessed that in the last part of the 1940s and mid 1950s, 350,000 individuals were cleansed from the party, 150,000 were detained, and 2,000 were executed. Rákosi was viewed as one of the most devoted to Stalin amongst

the area's despots, and his reign was a bleak crossroads in Hungary's set of experiences. A period of savagery and tyranny during the 1930s and 1940s had been supplanted a significantly more fierce dictatorship.

Amongst those designated by the system was János Kádár. Brought into the world in 1912, Kádár had joined the socialists as a young and ascended the positions of the party mechanical assembly before the Second World War. During the contention, he expected a place of authority prior to being detained by the Nazis. As with such countless other conspicuous socialist pioneers like Stalin and Romanian pioneer Nicolae Ceausescu, Kádár had the option to further develop his profession possibilities through his powerful organisztional capacities and his expertise in exploring bureaucracy.

In 1948, Kádár was selected Minister of the Interior by Rákosi, in this way supervising the preliminary of Laszlo Rajk.[22] Again, in ordinary Stalinist style, after Rákosi had involved Kádár in the Rajk case, he then, at that point, directed his concentration toward the Minister of the Interior himself. Compelled to leave in 1950 for health reasons, Kádár had to remain in his very own show preliminary, blamed for spying for the Horthy system. After the typical shallow court procedures, Kádár was condemned to life detainment, remembering a period for isolation. Delivered after Stalin's demise and Rákosi's expulsion from power in 1954, Kádár would arise as a significant player in Hungarian governmental issues, remembering for the result of the 1956 uprising.

One of the center explanations behind every one of the cleanses during this period was the pressure among Stalin and Yugoslav pioneer Josif Broz Tito. The inconveniences among Stalin and Tito happened because of strains inside the Cominform, the global Communist Information Bureau. The association, framed in 1947, was a committee of socialist systems and gatherings under the careful focus of the Soviets, however Tito was one of a handful of the socialist chiefs who had critical authenticity with his kin because of his activities as a hardliner chief during the conflict. It was a proportion of this renown that Belgrade was made the foundation of the Comintern in 1947. It was additionally a genuine embarrassment for Stalin when Tito supposedly challenged Soviet authority inside the socialist world.

Tito

Tito's mentality towards international strategy was the impetus for the conflict inside the Comintern, and regardless of his later standing for a more safe type of communism. During the common conflict in Greece, which constrained the Americans to figure the Truman Doctrine, Tito took a more extreme line than Stalin. This might have been on the grounds that, as a conflict time sectarian, Tito identified with the Greek left-wing hardliners. Tito then, at that point, needed to send troops to Albania when agitation happened there, and he even discussed a proper consolidation with socialist Bulgaria.

his would be the last bit of excess that will be tolerated for Stalin, who looked to get control over the Yugoslav chief. The Soviet tyrant trusted himself, with some defense, to be the unopposed head of the socialist world. Furthermore, Stalin had additionally learned through experience when he figured mediation may animate a Western reaction, something he was quick to stay away from in the Balkans. Stalin's essential objective in the early long periods of the Cold War was to frame a progression of client support states on the boundaries of the Soviet Union, and Tito's activities compromised a Western reaction, which Stalin would not tolerate.

As a result, he summoned Tito's two lieutenants, Edvard Kardelj and Milovan Djilas, to Moscow. Dissatisfied with the Yugoslav response, Stalin expelled the country from the Cominform on June 28, 1948.[23] Though it issued an invitation to Tito and his top lieutenants to attend, Tito refused to travel there, noting that "if we have to be killed, we'll be killed on our own
soil." That was a reasonable knowledge, given Stalin's long history of calling individuals to regions he controlled to have them killed.

hus, for quite some time, Yugoslavia existed in a kind of vacuum, with the Soviet Union approaching over it in fury. Tito previously looked towards the Americans, confused by the whole undertaking, to save him from the USSR, proclaiming, "The Americans are not fools. They will not allow the Russians to arrive at the Adriatic." This basically typified Tito's unfamiliar and homegrown arrangement for the remainder of his rule as Yugoslavia's domineering president – keeping a types of socialist state while depending on implicit Western help to keep the Soviet juggernaut under control. Edvard Kardelj, Yugoslavia's Foreign Minister, given a concise synopsis of how his country could keep up with itself as an unaligned state between the two huge power coalitions of the
twentieth century: by utilizing the "inclination among the colonialists to take advantage of the inconsistencies between the communist states, especially similarly as we wish to take advantage of the inward inconsistencies of the radical system."

The U.S. what's more England mindfully embraced a "wedge procedure" towards Yugoslavia, supporting it to keep it out of the Soviet effective reach and set up a barrier in the method of Stalin's European desires. Tito in like manner stopped giving guide to the Greek socialist associations, taken care of U.S. Loan Lease help, and compensated English and American individuals whose property in Yugoslavia had endured seizure. All things considered, the Americans normally stayed careful of Tito's and Yugoslavia's aims. They likewise couldn't exactly choose how to manage a country that housed an abusive, oppressive Marxist system, at this point gave solid indications of patriotism and showed itself able to resist the still-ascendant force of Moscow. As George Frost Kennan, a compelling

Cold War political tactician, said of Yugoslavia, "another element of crucial and significant importance has been brought into the world socialist development by the demonstration

that the Kremlin can be effectively resisted by one of its own cronies. By 1955, the American government had given Tito more than $1.2 billion in consolidated monetary and military guide. The British likewise gave help, however on a lesser scale because of their fading power, and Tito's system step by step created some distance from an absolutely socialist methodology as the even minded requests of endurance set viability in front of ideology.

Tito was even worried that the Red Army may attack his country. Truth be told, Stalin moved the central command of the Cominform from Belgrade to Bucharest, yet his methodology separated from that was to dispatch a supported mission of hostile to Yugoslav propaganda.[24]

Stalin massed Soviet soldiers on the Yugoslav boundary in 1949 in Hungary, yet he was subsequently occupied by the episode of the Korean War. In any case, these occasions would have an effect in Hungary. To be named as a Titoist was to be marked a freak and gone against to the partisan division in Moscow. An allegation of Titoism, one of Rákosi's beloved gadgets, was a risky claim for sure. The Hungarian specialists seemed to delight in looking for out
itoists, even after Stalin's death.[25]

The Stalin-Tito split had two further ramifications for the remainder of the socialist world. In the first place, it implied that any further shows of freedom would probably be managed quickly and cruelly by Moscow. This was the setting to what exactly unfolded when East Berliners ascended in 1953 and, considerably more essentially, for the 1956 Hungarian Uprising. Second, Tito's breakaway gave him tremendous validity across both the socialist and popularity based world. It offered an alternate model of communism, and it gave desire to others that nations could step a more independent way between the two superpower circles of influence.

eanwhile, as in practically every country that embraced communist measures during the Cold War, Hungary's expectations for everyday comforts before long started to deteriorate. The country's socialist system

forced difficulties on a large portion of the Hungarian populace from 1949
onwards, and the nature of living declined until 1953.
[26]

The whole locale, in any case, was offered a chance of life upon the
demise of Stalin in 1953. After right around 30 years in power, Stalin had
cut a wrap of dread across his own nation prior to incurring comparable
dread across Central and

Eastern Europe. A large part of the psychotic mentalities that included
socialist systems across the area mirrored the mannerisms of Stalin
himself, and the distrustfulness and absence of sympathy or leniency were
borne out even in the despot's demise. In spite of not hearing from Stalin
for a really long time, his gatekeepers were too hesitant to even consider
upsetting the Soviet chief, notwithstanding the reality he'd experienced a
stroke. The interruption in calling for crisis treatment might well have
been crucial.

f the smothering climate in the district typified the ghost of Stalin, then,
at that point, his demise permitted breathing space, and surprisingly some
novel plans to circulate.
ithin weeks, a significant number of the jails of the Gulag framework had
been exhausted, and even inside the Soviet Union itself a power battle
occurred between Nikita Khrushchev, Georgy Malenkov, and Lavrenti
Beria. All choices proposed the chance of change at home and abroad.

The first part of the Communist Bloc where this was put to the test was
East Berlin in June 1953, just a few months after Stalin's death. The
chaos was triggered by disgruntled workers going on strike and being
joined by civilians angry about shortages.[27] Under pressure from the
Soviet military, the East German government cracked down on the
protestors, jailing thousands and even killing some during and after the
demonstrations.[28]

The Hungarian Uprising

Instead of going about as an obstruction to would-be reformers, occasions
in Berlin simply appeared to animate comparable activities, first in Poland
and afterward in Hungary. At this point, Hungarians had become baffled
with Mátyás Rákosi's pitiless and clumsy time in office. It was to some
help in this way that he was pushed from power in July 1953, apparently on
the grounds that the new Soviet leadership

disapproved of his draconian methods.[29] Coming a month after the protests in East Berlin, his removal from power allowed Imre Nagy to become leader.
[30]

Nagy

Born in 1896, Imre Nagy was a long lasting socialist and, fairly amusingly considering the coming occasions, was propelled to join the socialists following the 1917 Bolshevik Revolution. Nagy had a long vocation as a Communist Party apparatchik, both in Hungary and the Soviet Union, including for the dreaded Soviet mystery police, the NKVD. Awkwardly for the people who later lauded Nagy's part in the 1956 Uprising, he was fundamental to the removal of ethnic Germans in the outcome of the Second World War. Truth be told, Nagy held onto some enthusiastic senses which went to the front during the occasions of 1956.

When he succeeded Matyas Rákosi in 1953, Nagy decreased the degrees of constraint and endeavor to plot another course in financial approach. Inside a short space of time, the air in Hungary, one of the most abusive in the Communist Bloc, became less oppressive under Nagy. The new Hungarian pioneer endeavored to plot a new, more moderate course, here and there homogeneous with the monetary changes proposed by Moscow.

Nevertheless, Rákosi actually employed impact in the Politburo, where different hardliners were despondent with regards to the bearing of Nagy's arrangements. Nagy additionally clearly went excessively far in any event, for the obviously change disapproved of Khrushchev,

so he was dismissed in April 1955 and compelled to sit on the sidelines.

Dissent began to mix after the hole of the "Secret Speech," one of the more questionable scenes of the Cold War. Whenever he had hardened his power, Khrushchev needed to manage the memory of his dead archetype. Beria's absolution program had brought about a large number of political detainees getting back with stories of the unforgiving, cruel conditions in Stalin's Gulag. As bits of gossip about Stalin's abominations and maltreatments of force started to spread through the populace, Khrushchev came to accept that the power of the Party was compromised, since the genuine degree of Stalin's violations was becoming known as more examinations uncovered more data. Simultaneously, Khrushchev accepted that renouncing Stalinism would support the fortunes of the Party and rouse steadfastness among the people.

eginning in October 1955, Khrushchev started to battle to inform agents to the impending twentieth Party Congress concerning the maltreatments of the previous ruler. He got resistance, especially from Molotov and Malenkov, however Khrushchev continued. Different pioneers at long last concurred, yet got Khrushchev to consent to give his comments to a shut session.

The twentieth Party Congress opened on February 14, 1956. Khrushchev opened with comments that contained hidden reactions of Stalin. Nothing more was said concerning Stalin, notwithstanding, until the finish of the Congress. In the early morning of February 25, Soviet agents were told to go to an uncommon early morning shut meeting of the Congress; unfamiliar correspondents and onlookers from Communist Parties in different countries were avoided. What happened throughout the following four hours was a discourse by Khrushchev entitled On the Cult of Personality and Its Consequences. It became referred to history as the "Secret Speech."

Before a stunned crowd, Khrushchev deliberately destroyed Stalin's standing. He started by expressing unequivocally that there was no doubt about the late ruler's commitments in the Revolution, the Civil War, and in developing the financial arrangement of the Soviet Union. However, he proceeded to say, a clique of character had developed around Stalin, helped and abetted by Stalin himself; such a character religion disregarded the actual standards of Marxist-Leninism.   From there, he moved to Lenin's own assertions on Stalin: "[Lenin] distinguished in Stalin in time those negative attributes which came about later in grave outcomes. Dreading the future destiny of the party and

of the Soviet country, VI Lenin made a totally right portrayal of Stalin. He called attention to that it was important to consider moving Stalin from the situation of general secretary since Stalin was unreasonably discourteous, didn't have a legitimate demeanor toward his companions, and was eccentric and mishandled his power."

Khrushchev depicted the manner by which Stalin continued to merge his power after Stalin's demise: "Stalin acted not through influence, clarification and patient collaboration with individuals, however by forcing his ideas and requesting outright accommodation to his viewpoint. Whoever went against these ideas or attempted to demonstrate his [own] perspective and the accuracy of his [own] position was ill-fated to expulsion from the administration aggregate and to resulting moral and actual obliteration. This was particularly evident during the period following the seventeenth party congress, when numerous unmistakable party pioneers and typical party laborers, legitimate and committed to the reason for socialism, succumbed to Stalin's despotism."

While Khrushchev allowed that Stalin put down certified dangers to Marxism-Leninism in the Soviet Union (like supporters of Trotsky), he called attention to that once such dangers had been managed, Stalin before long turned his sights "against numerous genuine socialists, against those party units who had borne the substantial heap of the common conflict and the first and most troublesome long periods of industrialization and collectivization, who had battled effectively against the Trotskyites and the conservatives for the Leninist party line."

Stalin started the idea "foe of individuals." This term consequently made it pointless that the philosophical blunders of a man or men occupied with a contention be demonstrated. It utilized the cruelest constraint, abusing all standards of progressive legitimateness, against any individual who in any capacity couldn't help contradicting Stalin, against the people who were just associated with threatening purpose, against the people who had terrible notorieties. The idea "foe of individuals" really disposed of the chance of any sort of philosophical battle or the creation of one's perspectives known on either issue, even [issues] of a pragmatic sort. All in all, the main verification of responsibility really utilized, against all standards of current lawful science, was simply the "admission" of the charged. As resulting testing has demonstrated, "admissions" were gained through actual tensions against the denounced. This prompted glaring infringement of progressive lawfulness and to the way that numerous altogether guiltless people - [persons] who in the past hosted protected the gathering line - became

victims.

hrushchev then, at that point, continued, over the course of the following a few hours, to efficiently destroy the Stalin fantasy. He definite the suppression of some prominent Bolsheviks; scrutinized a portion of Stalin's choices during the Second World War; and noticed the numerous appearances of the Stalin character clique (place names, melodies, and so forth) He wrapped up by expressing, "Companions! The twentieth congress of the Communist coalition of the Soviet Union has showed with another strength the unwavering solidarity of our party, its cohesiveness around the focal panel, its undaunted will to achieve the incredible errand of building socialism. Furthermore the way that we present in the entirety of their implications the essential issues of conquering the clique of the person which is strange to Marxism-Leninism, just as the issue of selling its oppressive outcomes, is proof of the extraordinary moral and political strength of our party. We are sure beyond a shadow of a doubt that our party, furnished with the chronicled goals of the twentieth Congress, will lead the Soviet individuals along the Leninist way to new triumphs, to new triumphs. Long experience the triumphant flag of our party - Leninism!"

Khrushchev

Before the Secret Speech spilled, there were not many public exhibitions of distress against the socialist system in Hungary. The solitary exemption came after the nation's loss in the 1954 soccer World Cup Final.[31] The alleged "Strong Magyars," drove by soccer legend Ferenc Puskás, had gone unbeaten for a considerable length of time before the competition, so the loss against West
Germany, as of late the involving power in the nation, was hence an unpleasant reality. It is likewise a sign of what mixed the interests of Hungarians in the mid 1950s.

However, the international climate was additionally moving during the 1950s. While the Soviet Union and the United States stayed antagonistic, the West began to fabricate joins with nations like Hungary who were frantic for exchange relations outside the Communist Bloc. One of the vital occasions to impact the district was the course of the Secret Speech, which shocked

Khrushchev's partners and debilitated help for socialism globally, just as cultivating the significant split in the socialist world among China and the USSR.

because of the discourse, party initiatives started getting away from the Stalinist projects they had recently used, and suppression was by and large loose. For the populaces in Central and Eastern Europe, it additionally implied that the authenticity of Soviet-upheld socialism was debilitated and immediately prompted fights. At the point when the substance of the discourse spilled, it was spread as
publicity by the US's Radio Free Europe.[32]

In June 1956, workers protested their conditions in the Polish city of Poznań, calling for "bread, liberty and freedom,"[33] but after three days of strikes, the authorities stepped in to violently repress them, leading to 74 deaths and many more casualties. Crucially, Khrushchev himself flew to Poland and told the socialists he would not permit the nation to split away from the Bloc. He upheld up the danger by preparing Soviet soldiers.

nce more, as in East Berlin in 1953, this didn't discourage individuals from exhibiting somewhere else. Truth be told, the occasions in Poland went about as impetus for the more genuine fights in Hungary four months after the fact. To be sure, the Hungarians cheered up from the way that the new Polish pioneer, Władysław Gomułka, was eventually left set up by the Soviets in the midst of enormous group demonstrations.

**Gomul
ka**

   As the Secret Speech spilled and the Nagy government responded, it reflected the movements inside the Soviet Union itself by delivering political detainees and concentrating on the economy, including the stockpile of buyer goods.[34] Even leaving to the side Stalin's passing, in more extensive terms, Stalinist systems had been sabotaged by the conspicuous disappointments of their economic strategies, mishandled industrialization programs, and an overall environment of restraint and uncertainty.[35]

   Although socialist veterans like Nagy offered any desire for an alternate future, the power vacuum all through the locale likewise welcomed protesters to have a special interest, and this began in Hungary with understudy gatherings. The turmoil proceeded into the pre-winter, and in one of the most clear instances of a split with the past, on October 6, 1956, László Rajk was reburied in the midst of a passionate function went to by 10,000 Hungarians. This was one more component worth noting, because the demonstrations of the 1950s and 1960s within the Communist Bloc were often pushed by the far left, with socialists criticizing other socialists. It certainly seemed odd that a hardline communist such as Rajk, who had helped establish the Hungarian secret police, was now being eulogized as an alternative to the likes of Rákosi. Nevertheless, the reburial undermined Rákosi's ongoing influence on the government and paved the way for further demonstrations.[36]

Events came to a head on October 23, 1956 when a number of spontaneous demonstrations took place in Budapest.[37] The demands from the crowds included free speech, the dissolution of the secret police, and the end of Soviet influence, political and military.[38] Pictures of Imre Nagy were held aloft by the protestors, and he was summoned to the national assembly, where he gave a speech aimed at the Communist Party. For the Hungarian crowds, however, the issues now even transcended leftwing ideology, which seemingly did little for most of the population. The calls of the 1956
dissidents presently moved a more nationalistic way. Devoted tunes and mottos were recited, and the groups started to expand. Hungarians merged on Budapest, with around 200,000 accepted to have come out in the city on October 23.

The socialist initiative transmission a revilement of the fights, calling for calm and for the protestors to remain down, however this main kindled issues. The sculpture of Stalin, which had been raised five years sooner in the focal point of Budapest, was destroyed, and swarms endeavored to storm the Hungarian Radio structure trying to peruse out their requests on the wireless transmissions. The Hungarian specialists turned out to be progressively restless to stifle the fights, utilizing poisonous gas to dispense the groups. This main exacerbated the situation, as vehicles were set land and the savagery gave off an impression of being heightening. Significantly more shockingly, security powers shipped off suppress the aggravations really agreed with the dissenters now and again. It looked like Hungary was nearly a revolution.

A picture of a Hungarian flag being placed on the ruins of the Stalin

statue

ith occasions apparently spiraling crazy, the Hungarian socialist authority mentioned military help from Moscow to end the uprising and reimpose peace and lawfulness. Socialist Faction Secretary Ernő Gerő composed with the USSR's most incredible military pioneer, Marshal Georgy Zhukov, who requested Soviet powers into Hungary the next day, October 24.

When the Soviets showed up, be that as it may, they were met by equipped Hungarian opposition - regular people had raged weapons storage spaces and had shaped volunteer armies. Seeing Soviet tanks moving into the capital city, some being situated before the public parliament, was shocking to Hungarians, and many waged war thus. Irregulars set up blockades around the city, watching key crossing points and surprisingly figured out how to assume responsibility for the radio structure. The Hungarian armed force that was as yet faithful to the system terminated on a portion of the nonconformists, and they returned fire in different spots. Soviet soldiers likewise became involved, however at first, all sides pulled their punches.

A picture of Hungarian protesters on October 25

An image of Hungarian officers being cheered by a crowd

Other aggravations were accounted for in different urban communities around the nation, yet the battling was all things considered amassed in Budapest, and most importantly, shooting between all sides occurred outside the parliament working in Budapest. This really hurried the breakdown of the system, with Ernő Gerő escaping the country to the USSR and preparing for Imre Nagy and János Kádár to dominate. Both called for quiet and a finish to the fighting.

Meanwhile, civilian armies began to all the more forcefully assault the Red Army and individuals from the socialist foundation, including known or associated individuals with the mysterious police and party functionaries. As this recommended, the battling was going in a more ruthless and rough course, and public watchman units drove by hostile to socialist previous armed force official Béla Király, who had spent the post-World War II years in jail, were especially significant in this respect.

as anyone might expect, these activities prompted responses by the possessing troops, and the Soviet armed force battled against the Hungarian irregulars for four days before they started somewhat pulling out from Budapest. Nagy had facilitated a truce, and Moscow gave Nagy, presently state head, the chance to bring back the power of the Hungarian Communist Party.

Instead, Nagy supported the dissenters' requests, and a progression of radio stations gave the progressives trust that Nagy was for sure facing the Soviets and paying attention to their interests. It presently seemed as though a completely fledged insurgency was occurring. Progressive boards and gatherings were framing, taking extremist perspectives on the country's past the state of affairs as a component of the Soviet Bloc. It was the sort of example that had happened in socialist transformations, for example, in Russia in 1917, however this time it was an insurgency against socialism, which had been forced on Hungarians in spite of some leftover help for leftwing approaches. What most blended Hungarian enthusiasm and the reaction in 1956 was the feeling that the nation had no office of its own and that it was basically a satellite state, even province, of the Soviet Union. The dissatisfaction about this situation, which had clearly stewed throughout recent years, bubbled over toward the finish of October.

Meanwhile, backlashes kept on being done against the mysterious police and any similarity to Soviet impact. Obviously, things were not continuing as Moscow had envisioned when it hauled its soldiers out only days prior - the Soviets had accepted, incorrectly, that by introducing the more "liberal" Nagy in power, he could placate the Hungarian "crooks." It was maybe characteristic of the post-Stalin system, which was reflexively (albeit

just imperceptibly) more open to mollification, however it was going to demonstrate that it could rapidly return to the old methods of oppression.

truth be told, the brutality dispensed against supportive of Soviet numbskulls in Hungary was subsequently refered to by Moscow as motivation to assume responsibility for the country forcibly, and notwithstanding its proclivity for trickery and promulgation, the Soviets were not off-base when they said that savagery was occurring. Socialist "red stars" were destroyed from public structures, and party perusing materials were scorched and obliterated. Various volunteer army and military figures arose, drove by people like Pál Maléter, József Dudás and Béla Király, and it is assessed that in excess of 200 party apparatchiks were executed.

A picture of an executed party member

An image of harm done to the party headquarters

Nagy was presently the pioneer, but accidentally, of the Hungarian Revolution. On October 30, 1956, he framed an alliance government, ostensibly public socialist. Understanding a further Soviet intercession was reasonable, Nagy endeavored to decouple his country from the Communist Bloc by pronouncing impartiality and basically pulling out Hungary from the Warsaw Pact. Nagy figured he could impersonate the situation of Austria in the Cold War,

moving to one of neutrality,[39] however he was additionally mindful that the Soviet soldiers that pulled out from Budapest had not left the country. The battling may have halted on October 28, yet Soviet powers were situated in provincial regions outside the nation, and there was little uncertainty that more military units were holding on to enter Hungary if needed.

agy engaged the worldwide local area, including Western nations, for help in repulsing the Soviets and requesting acknowledgment of the country's new circumstance. Nagy wrote to United Nations Secretary-General Dag Hammarskjöld that he had "ended the Warsaw Pact, pronounced the lack of bias of Hungary and mentioned the United Nations to ensure the impartiality of the country." He likewise educated Hammarskjöld that "enormous Soviet military units crossed the line of the nation, walking toward Budapest.
They possess rail line lines, rail route stations, and railroad wellbeing equipment.

Reports likewise have come that Soviet military developments an east-west way are being seen on the region of Western Hungary." Nagy at long last called "upon the incredible powers to perceive the nonpartisanship of Hungary and request that the Security Council educate the Soviet and Hungarian legislatures to begin the exchanges quickly." obviously, that was never liable to succeed given that the USSR had a denial on the Security Council.
Ultimately, the UN investigated the occasions in Hungary, yet not until after the residue was at that point settling.

he hug of the uprising by Nagy was unsafe, and he probably realized it was probably going to draw a serious Soviet reaction. Nagy's bet was that external powers, the West or the worldwide local area all the more indistinctly, would go to Hungary's guide. He tended to the now overjoyed public by saying, "The public authority sentences the perspectives as per which the present imposing development is a counter-transformation," saying this was "an incredible, public and vote based development, embracing and binding together the entirety of our kin." He likewise let them know that he had laid out the objectives of "ensuring our public opportunity, autonomy, and power, of propelling our general public, our financial and political framework in transit of majority rules system." Nagy announced that he would carry out "the simply requests of individuals," cancel the state
security benefits, and haggle with the USSR on troop withdrawals.[40] While the United States offered some expository help for Hungary because of this, the Americans would not coordinate with the caring words with any material support.

On November 3, apparently confronting an inevitable Soviet assault, Nagy reshuffled his administration by acquiring different groups, including the Independent Smallholder's Party, and decreasing the socialists to a minority. Meanwhile, Khrushchev had ventured out to other Warsaw Pact nations to illuminate them he expected to smash the Hungarian Uprising. The Soviet Politburo had met on November 1 and chosen to utilize military power to assume back responsibility for the country.

That timetable clarifies that Nagy's endeavors to cut out an autonomous way were purposeless during the break in threats, however strangely, the Soviet Ambassador to Hungary, Yuri Andropov, gave confirmations to

Nagy that the Soviets would not attack a subsequent time. Indeed, Andropov even seemed to submit to Hungary's requests of UN intervention to get the country's

nonpartisanship and the withdrawal of the excess unfamiliar soldiers. It was probable an unpleasant reality for Nagy to swallow when he learned only hours after the fact that Andropov's assertion was meaningless.

On November 4, 1956, Red Army reenforcements spilled across the Hungarian boundary and into Budapest, and in an overwhelming demonstration of solidarity, the Soviets repressed the uprising and any demonstration of opposition. Prior to the primary mediation, on October 23, there had been five Soviet divisions positioned in the country. On November 4, the strength of the Soviet armed force was completely 17 divisions, which gave overpowering prevalence. Codenamed "Activity Whirlwind," troops were conveyed from the Carpathian locale, making scramble towards the Hungarian capital. The choice might have been marginally postponed fully expecting hardliners possibly holding onto control inside Hungary itself. Later records propose that an "interior arrangement" was for sure on the table, led
by the old Stalinist group inside the party.[41] This example would rehash the same thing a fourth of a century under comparable conditions in Poland, when General Jaruzelski organized an upset and proclaimed military law as opposed to having Soviet soldiers attack the country.

In the early long stretches of November 4, Budapest was totally encircled by Soviet soldiers. Under the front of obscurity, tanks moved into the city and assaulted Hungarian military positions, for example, armed force dormitory. The Red Army even utilized air backing and strikes to hit chosen targets. The Hungarian public, who only days before had accepted that they may really appreciate opportunity, woke up to the hints of gunfire, mortar shells, and explosions.
The Soviets even sent a portion of their cutting edge T-54 tanks.

The Hungarians settled on frantic decisions for help from the West, however no help was forthcoming.[42] That day, as Soviet soldiers moved into the capital, Budapest Radio settled on wild eyed decisions for outside help, with one transmission broadly approaching individuals to "help Hungary...Help, help, help…
Civilized individuals of the world. On the watch pinnacle of 1,000-year

old Hungary the last flares start to go out. Soviet tanks and firearms are thundering over Hungarian soil. Our ladies - moms and girls - are sitting in dread.
They still have terrible memories of the army's entry in 1945. Save our souls…this word may be the last from the last Hungarian freedom station. Listen to our call. Help us - not with advice, not with words, but with action, with soldiers and arms."[43]

A picture of Soviet T-54 tanks in Budapest

An image of harmed Soviet tanks in Budapest

While the Hungarian powers never gotten an opportunity, the Hungarian armed force and

local armies set up obstruction the nation over, most strikingly in Budapest and the city of Pécs. It is assessed that somewhere close to 10,000 and 15,000 warriors and contenders struggled the attack. Obviously, few out of every odd Hungarian trooper endeavored to stand up to. Seeing the status quo going, some immediately situated themselves, either out of practicality or genuine opinion, as favorable to Soviet. This was especially valid for the top of the food chain and politicians.

itnesses said Soviet soldiers killed currently injured individuals and hauled bodies around the roads of Budapest with their tanks as a deterent against additional dissent, however the Hungarians kept on battling. One piece of Budapest specifically became famous for the demonstration of fortitude and resistance against the Red Army: Corvin Passage. Situated in the focal point of Budapest close to Budapest Radio station and the military dormitory, the tight entry was an essential chokepoint where a basically resident or guerilla armed force endeavored opposition against

the unfathomably bigger and better prepared Soviet powers, which
numbered somewhere in the range of 75,000 and 200,000. Corvin
Passage had been set up in the uprising of October 24 and was
immediately protected again after November 4.
Although exact data is hard to get, verifiable appraisals have
recommended that somewhere close to 1,000 and 4,000 Hungarians
battled at Corvin Passage against the Soviets during the uprising.

While at first the local armies at Corvin Passage were confused and
impromptu, as time advanced, they really became coordinated with the
Hungarian military in battling against the Soviet soldiers. First László
Iván Kovács and afterward Gergely Pongrátz drove the powers at Corvin
Passage until the uprising was at long last subdued on November 9. The
Hungarian irregulars at Corvin Passage utilized guerilla strategies,
Molotov mixed drinks, and expert sharpshooter fire from skyscraper
vantage focuses in the close by structures. This obviously was an
exceptionally assymetric circumstance, as the Hungarians were utilizing
essential strategies against cannons and mortar fire.

Inevitably, the rearguard activity at Corvin Passage could just keep
going so long, and the Red Army at last crushed the region with their
prevalent capability. The setback numbers are obscure at Corvin Passage,
yet it is accepted that a considerable lot of the heads of the opposition here
figured out how to escape over the line to Austria after the uprising had
been put down.

lsewhere, the vast majority of the Hungarian irregulars and military
acknowledged before long the Soviets attacked on November 4 that
obstruction was self-destructive. Indeed, the
military was requested to come into line once a new, supportive of
Soviet government was set up. Another administration was introduced
with the Red Army actually battling in the city, known as the
"Hungarian Revolutionary Worker Peasant Government." Ironically, it
was driven by Nagy's past partner, János Kádár. Numerous Hungarians
came to consider Kádár to be a supportive of Moscow numbskull and a
deceiver against the enthusiastic uprising, while less basic voices
accepted Kádár was simply tolerating the inescapable and was basically
a pragmatist who exchanged sides since he thought there could have
been no other valid option.

Kádár

Either way, when the Hungarian Uprising was finished, the Soviets had shown that even with a more safe pioneer than somebody like Stalin in the Kremlin, they would not endure any contradiction inside their range of authority. Hungary represented the primary genuine test to Soviet standard since the finish of World War II, and the Soviets created an object lesson using the defiant country.

The Legacy of the Uprising

The disappointment of the Hungarian Uprising was one more illustration of how Hungary had been sold out by the extraordinary powers. It had occurred after the First World War, after the Second World War, and presently after an unrest invigorated by a grassroots dissent that began with a demonstration of distress against the Soviet-upheld socialist system. A few appraisals propose that around 20,000 individuals were

killed during the uprising, and around 200,000 fled
the country, essentially across the boundary with Austria.[44] The loss
numbers are very bleak considering the uprising was over after a couple
days.

of course, the kickback would endure significantly longer than the
concise upheaval. The battling had come about in around 700 dead Soviets
and another 1,500 injured, which exhibited the strength of against Soviet
opinion in the area. While different spots in the Communist Bloc may
have been more suppressed, the Soviets needed to stress that such
sentiments hid underneath somewhere else and could rise over without
warning. The draconian crackdown was as much a message to the
remainder of the Communist Bloc as it was the fretful Hungarians
themselves.

One of the key reasons the Soviets acted so ruthlessly was that
worldwide consideration was redirected somewhere else in October and
November 1956 because of the Suez Crisis. Hungarian progressives would
later put their bombed uprising on the British and French, and their
blundered endeavors to force their will on Egypt. The emergency revolved
around the Suez Canal, one of the veins of world exchange and vital in
interfacing Britain's process for general stores and provinces. Subsequent
to applying authority over North Africa for a really long time, Britain and
France were step by step compelled to pull out from the area after the
Second World War. In Egypt, the most crowded country in North Africa,
an overthrow in 1952 expelled the ruler and introduced a gathering of
armed force officials. Ultimately, Gamal Abdel Nasser would arise as the
nation's chief and embrace Arab patriotism, and as a feature of this system,
he tried to nationalize the Suez Canal, then, at that point, run by an
European-claimed privately owned business. This insulted the French and
British, who had recently had little issue in compelling the Egyptians to do
their offering. Subsequently, they incubated an arrangement with the
Israelis, who might attack the waterway zone and afterward get support
from the French and British. The arrangement was executed on October
29, 1956, squarely in the center of the Hungarian Uprising. The affection
of the Suez plan was plain for

all to see, however how much the Eisenhower organization stood up
against its partners was astonishing. Under tension from Washington, the

French and British had to pull out. Lamentably for the Hungarians, this implied that when Soviet tanks moved into Hungary on November 4 to smash the uprising, undeniably less consideration was paid than in any case would have been the case.

n the repercussions of the uprising, Kádár managed what was metaphorically named "standardization" approaches. Actually, this implied stifling difference, detaining or executing the instigators of the revolt, and managing a time of quiet. Some irregular strikes proceeded contrary to the new system, yet Kádár stifled those through power, imprisoning more than 20,000 and executing somewhere in the range of 200 and 300.

The most notorious preliminary was that of Imre Nagy himself. Nagy had at first attempted to track down shelter in the Yugoslav government office, a country that successfuuly extricated Moscow's grasp in the last part of the 1940s, however he was in the long run captured.
Tried covertly on the charge of treachery, Nagy was executed in June 1958. Moscow obviously needed to make an impression on different forerunners in the Communist Bloc what might befall the individuals who veered off, however for Hungarians, Nagy turned into an enthusiastic martyr.

lthough the worldwide reaction was quieted because of occasions in Suez, when the accounts arose of what had occurred in Hungary, there was far reaching shock. In Western nations, the cachet of leftwing developments and socialist coalitions were lethally harmed both by Khrushchev's "Secret Speech" and the attack of Hungary. The Soviet intrusion of Hungaray was likewise a promulgation debacle for Moscow, and it would be deteriorated by comparable occasions in Czechoslovakia in 1968. Albeit Western mediations in places like Vietnam likewise drew inescapable harshness, by the last part of the 1980s it was generally recognized that the West had won the moral argument.

The reaction of both the Soviets and the West, or absence of it, additionally had an impact. Occasions in Hungary proposed that European states were powerless against Soviet underhandedness making or altogether obstruction. Western Germany, for instance, was given a reasonable illustration into what may befall it on the off chance that was likewise uncovered. Subsequently, West German Chancellor Konrad Adenauer solidified Bonn's NATO strategy and brought the nation well and really under

America's nuclear weapons umbrella.[45] It would cause many domestic

issues, however Hungary's destiny in 1956 set West Germany's situation in the Western Bloc, and accordingly it established the division of Europe.

Kádár's constraint proceeded until the mid 1960s, yet after that his system grew more in the style of a harmless autocracy. Hungary stayed a one-party state until the last part of the 1980s, yet it was more open financially and politically than the majority of its friends, beside Yugoslavia. Kádár managed monetary changes during the 1960s like other socialist states, yet while most paddled back on advancement, Hungary persevered with its own "New Economic Mechanism."[46] As a result, the country was relatively more successful than other economies in the region.

Nevertheless, likewise with its peers, Hungary additionally thought that it is difficult to keep away from a time of stagnation beginning during the 1970s. Regardless of their earnest attempts to protect themselves from the industrialist world economy, nations in the Communist Bloc encountered the thump on effect of bigger monetary shocks. The oil value vacillations of the early and late 1970s are the best models, just as ware costs, taking off loan fees, and admittance to capital business sectors. The Hungarians endeavored to adjust to these shocks and without a doubt endured them more effectively than others.

Along with the monetary issues, nonconformist gatherings began to arise in Hungary during the 1970s and 1980s, albeit these were less coordinated than in Poland and Czechoslovakia.[47] Coupled with financial advancement, the disappointment that was so repressed in different pieces of the socialist world by the last part of the 1980s had some outlet in Hungary, just as somewhat higher living standards. In essence, Hungary and Poland were the most "liberal" communist regimes by the end of the 1980s.[48]

Kádár himself was removed in 1988. He was by then thought to be too solidified in his methodology as Soviet pioneer Mikhail Gorbachev's Glasnost and Perestroika strategies were clearing away the old thinking in the region.
Nevertheless, Hungary was one of only a handful of exceptional nations in Central and Eastern Europe that saw a tranquil progress to liberal vote based system in the last part of the 1980s and mid 1990s.

Once the Cold War was a relic of past times and Russia opened up a portion of the Soviet documents, numerous antiquarians have presumed that the 1956 Hungarian Uprising was the most genuine test to Soviet guideline in Central and Eastern

Europe during the entire Cold War.[49] The Soviets concocted a typically unlikely narrative to explain their actions, saying that the October 23 demonstrations had been hijacked by counterrevolutionary forces seeking to betray Hungarian socialism and sell the country out to the West. According to their line, only Soviet assistance for the real Hungarian patriots on November 4 could salvage the situation, but if anything, the Soviets implicitly conceded how threatened they were by the Hungarian Uprising in the way they dealt with subsequent unrest. They used the same playbook to respond to other uprisings, most notably in East Berlin in 1953 and Czechoslovakia in 1968.

Since the finish of the Cold War, Hungary has turned into a full individual from the European Union, NATO, and the Western group of countries. Monetary flourishing has been accomplished in stages and inconsistently, and absolutely there have been intense periods. The nation actually has thorny relationship with bigger abilities, for example in its relationship with the IMF after the 2008 monetary emergency and with the European Union after the 2015 exile crisis.
Moreover, the region lost in the Treaty of Trianon was not recuperated. By the by, Hungary has accomplished the self-assurance that the 1956 progressives battled for, and today the uprising is recalled in Hungary with October 23 filling in as a public occasion. Vacationers go to Budapest's "Place of Terror" to get a brief look at the valiance of, and cruel responses distributed to, those that tested socialist guideline and Soviet impact in Hungary.

Online Resources

Other books about 20th century history by Charles River

Editors Other books about Russian history by Charles River

Editors Other books about the Soviet invasion on Amazon

Bibliography

S.J. Ball, The Cold War: An International History 1947–1991

(London: Arnold, 1998)

BBC, "Soviet power in Eastern Europe," https://www.bbc.com/bitesize/guides/z9wxj6f/modification/2, [accessed 10 April 2019]

BBC Witness History, 'Hungarian Uprising of 1956,' 3 November 2011, https://www.bbc.co.uk/programs/p00ldxpv, [accessed 2 May 2019]

Laszlo Borhi, Hungary in the Cold War: 1945–1956 (Central European University Press, 2004)

Christopher Clark, The Sleepwalkers: How Europe Went to War in 1914 (London: Harper, 2014)

CNN, Cold War (TV Series, created by Jeremy Isaacs and Pat Mitchell, 1998)

Deutsche Welle, 'Holocaust casualties let go in Hungary,' 15 April 2016, https://www.dw.com/en/holocaust-casualties let go in-hungary/a-19192403

rzegorz Ekiert, The State Against Society: Political Crises and Their Aftermath in East Central Europe. (Princeton, N.J.: Princeton University Press; 1996)

Richard J. Evans, The Pursuit of Power: Europe 1815–1914 (London: Penguin, 2017)

Mary Fulbrook, History of Germany, 1918–2000: the separated nation (Oxford: Blackwell, 2002)

Robert Gerwarth, The Vanquished: Why the First World War Failed to End, 1917–1923 (London: Allen Lane, 2016)

Mark Gilbert, Cold War Europe: The Politics of a Contested Continent (Rowman and Littlefield, 2014)

Misha Glenny, The Balkans 1804–2012: Nationalism, War and the Great Powers (London: Granta, 2012)

The Guardian, 'Soviet tanks smash opposition,' 5 November 1956, https://www.theguardian.com/theguardian/1956/nov/05/fromthearchive1

Godfrey Hodgson, People's Century: From the beginning of the century to the night before the thousand years (Godalming: BBC Books, 1998)

Michael T. Kaufmann, 'Children of Communism,' The New York Times, 8 March 1987, https://www.nytimes.com/1987/03/08/magazine/the-children of-

communism.html, [accessed 2 May 2019]

aul Lendvai, One Day That Shook the Communist World: The 1956 Hungarian Uprising and Its Legacy, (Princeton University Press, 2008)

Bill Lomax, "The Hungarian upheaval of 1956 and the starting points of the Kádár system," Studies in Comparative Communism, 18:2/3 (1985, 87-113)

Kevin McDermott and Matthew Stibbe, The 1989 Revolutions in Central and Eastern Europe: From Communism to Pluralism (Manchester University Press, 2013)

Gorbachev Faults Stalin on Rift With Tito,' The New York Times 17 March 1988, https://www.nytimes.com/1988/03/17/world/gorbachev-deficiencies stalin-on-crack with-tito.html

Paul Preston, Coming of the Spanish Civil War: Reform, Reaction and Revolution in the Second Republic, (Taylor and Francis Group, 1994)

Jason Sharman, Repression and Resistance in Communist Europe (Routledge, 2003)

Thomas L. Sakmyster, Hungary's Admiral on Horseback: Miklós Horthy, 1918–1944 (Columbia University Press, 1993)

Brendan Simms, Europe: The Struggle for Supremacy 1453 to the Present
(London: Penguin, 2014)

US Department of State, "Articulation by Molotov" (Paris, 2 July 1947), Department of State (Ed.). A Decade of American Foreign Policy, Basic Documents 1941–1949. Washington: Department of State Printing Office, 1985.

Vladimir Tismaneanu, (ed.), 'Stalinism Revisited,' The Establishment of Communist Regimes in East-Central Europe. (Budapest, 2009, CEU

Press, pp. 231–254).

Stephen White, Communism and its Collapse (Routledge, 2002)

Gregory R. Witkowski, "Workers Revolt? Reconsidering the 17

June
Uprising in East Germany," German History, (24:2, 1 April 2006, pp. 243–266)Free Books by Charles River Editors

We have fresh out of the plastic new titles accessible for nothing most days of the week. To see which of our titles are at present free, click on this link.

Discounted Books by Charles River Editors

We have titles at a rebate cost of only 99 pennies regular. To see which of our titles are as of now 99 pennies, click on this link.

---

[1]Christopher Clark, The Sleepwalkers: How Europe Went to War in 1914 (London: Harper, 2014),
p. 450.
[2]Eugene Michail, 'Western Attitudes to War in the Balkans and the Shifting Meanings of
    Violence, 1912-1991,' Journal of Contemporary History, (47:219, 2012), pp. 219-241)), p. 220.
[3]obert Gerwarth, The Vanquished: Why the First World War Failed to End, 1917–1923
(London: Allen Lane, 2016)
[4]Robert Gerwarth, The Vanquished: Why the First World War Failed to End, 1917–1923
(London: Allen Lane, 2016)
[5]*Brendan Simms, Europe: The Struggle for Supremacy 1453 to the Present (London: Penguin, 2014)*
[6]*Brendan Simms, Europe: The Struggle for Supremacy 1453 to the Present (London: Penguin,
    2014), p. 313*
[7]Thomas L. Sakmyster, Hungary's Admiral on Horseback: Miklós Horthy, 1918–1944
    (Columbia University Press, 1993)
[8]*Paul Preston, Coming of the Spanish Civil War: Reform, Reaction and Revolution in the
    Second Republic, (Taylor and Francis Group, 1994)*

[9]Godfrey Hodgson, People's Century: From the beginning of the century to the night before the
    millennium(Godalming: BBC Books, 1998)
[10]   *isha Glenny, The Balkans 1804–2012: Nationalism, War and the Great Powers (London:
Granta, 2012)*
[11]   Deutsche Welle, 'Holocaust casualties let go in Hungary,' 15 April 2016,
    https://www.dw.com/en/holocaust-casualties let go in-hungary/a-19192403, [accessed 2 May
    2019]
[12]   *ason Sharman, Repression and Resistance in Communist Europe (Routledge, 2003), p. 69.*
[13]   *Stephen White, Communism and its Collapse (Routledge, 2002), p. 15.*

[14]   *Mark Gilbert, Cold War Europe: The Politics of a Contested Continent (Rowman and Littlefield, 2014), p. 29.*

[15]   *Jason Sharman, Repression and Resistance in Communist Europe (Routledge, 2003), p. 70.*

[16]   Godfrey Hodgson, People's Century: From the beginning of the century to the night before the millennium(Godalming: BBC Books, 1998)

[17]   Articulation by Molotov" (Paris, 2 July 1947), Department of State (Ed.). A Decade of American Foreign Policy, Basic Documents 1941–1949. Washington: Department of State Printing Office, 1985, https://www.cvce.eu/content/distribution/1999/1/1/f692bc11-0049-4b78-ba99-bc0ac81aedeb/publishable_en.pdf, got to 29 April 2019.

[18]   Godfrey Hodgson, The People's Century: From the beginning of the century to the night before the

[19]

[20]

thousand years (Godalming: BBC Books, 1998), p. 247.

[21]   BBC, "Soviet power in Eastern Europe," https://www.bbc.com/bitesize/guides/z9wxj6f/modification/2, [accessed 10 April 2019]

[22]   *Jason Sharman, Repression and Resistance in Communist Europe (Routledge, 2003), p. 70.*

[23]   Vladimir Tismaneanu, (ed.), 'Stalinism Revisited,' The Establishment of Communist Regimes in East-Central Europe. (Budapest, 2009, CEU Press, pp. 231–254).

[24]   Michael T. Kaufmann, 'Children of Communism,' The New York Times, 8 March 1987, https://www.nytimes.com/1987/03/08/magazine/the-children of-communism.html, [accessed 2 May 2019]

[25]   'Gorbachev Faults Stalin on Rift With Tito,' The New York Times 17 March 1988, https://www.nytimes.com/1988/03/17/world/gorbachev-shortcomings stalin-on-break with-tito.html, [accessed 3 September 2018]

[26]   'Gorbachev Faults Stalin on Rift With Tito,' The New York Times 17 March 1988, https://www.nytimes.com/1988/03/17/world/gorbachev-flaws stalin-on-fracture with-tito.html, [accessed 3 September 2018]

[27]   *Mark Gilbert, Cold War Europe: The Politics of a Contested Continent (Rowman and Littlefield, 2014), p. 55.*

[28]   *Jason Sharman, Repression and Resistance in Communist Europe (Routledge, 2003), p. 71.*

[29]   Gregory R. Witkowski, "Laborers Revolt? Rethinking the 17 June Uprising in East Germany," German History, (24:2, 1 April 2006, pp. 243–266), p. 263, Mary Fulbrook, History of Germany, 1918–2000: the partitioned country (Oxford: Blackwell, 2002), p. 155.

[30]   *Mary Fulbrook, History of Germany, 1918–2000: the partitioned country (Oxford: Blackwell, 2002), p. 155.*

[31]   CNN, Cold War (TV Series, delivered by Jeremy Isaacs and Pat Mitchell, 1998)

[32]   *Jason Sharman, Repression and Resistance in Communist Europe (Routledge, 2003), p. 71.*

[33]   *Paul Lendvai, One Day That Shook the Communist World: The 1956 Hungarian Uprising and Its Legacy, (Princeton University Press, 2008), p. 6.*

[34]   CNN, Cold War (TV Series, delivered by Jeremy Isaacs and Pat Mitchell, 1998)

[35]   CNN, Cold War (TV Series, created by Jeremy Isaacs and Pat Mitchell, 1998)

[36]   CNN, Cold War (TV Series, created by Jeremy Isaacs and Pat Mitchell, 1998)

[37]   Grzegorz Ekiert, The State Against Society: Political Crises and Their Aftermath in East Central Europe. (Princeton, N.J.: Princeton University Press; 1996), p. 45,

[38]   *Jason Sharman, Repression and Resistance in Communist Europe (Routledge, 2003), p. 72.*

[39]   *Paul Lendvai, One Day That Shook the Communist World: The 1956 Hungarian Uprising and Its Legacy, (Princeton University Press, 2008), p. 6.*

[40]   CNN, Cold War (TV Series, delivered by Jeremy Isaacs and Pat Mitchell, 1998)

[41]   CNN, Cold War (TV Series, created by Jeremy Isaacs and Pat Mitchell, 1998)

[42]   Bill Lomax, "The Hungarian upheaval of 1956 and the starting points of the Kádár system," Studies in Comparative Communism, 18:2/3 (1985, 87-113), p. 97.

[43]   Bill Lomax, "The Hungarian unrest of 1956 and the starting points of the Kádár system," Studies in Comparative Communism, 18:2/3 (1985, 87-113), p. 98.

[44]

[45]

[46]   Godfrey Hodgson, People's Century: From the beginning of the century to the night before the millennium(Godalming: BBC Books, 1998), p. 262.

[47]   he Guardian, 'Soviet tanks pound obstruction,' 5 November 1956, https://www.theguardian.com/theguardian/1956/nov/05/fromthearchive1

[48]   BBC Witness History, 'Hungarian Uprising of 1956,' 3 November 2011, https://www.bbc.co.uk/programs/p00ldxpv, [accessed 2 May 2019]

[49]   *S.J. Ball, The Cold War: An International History 1947–1991 (London: Arnold, 1998), p. 94.*

[50]   *Mark Gilbert, Cold War Europe: The Politics of a Contested Continent (Rowman and Littlefield, 2014), p. 143.*

[51]   Kevin McDermott and Matthew Stibbe, The 1989 Revolutions in Central and Eastern Europe: From Communism to Pluralism (Manchester University Press, 2013), p. 7.

[52]   evin McDermott and Matthew Stibbe, The 1989 Revolutions in Central and Eastern Europe: From Communism to Pluralism (Manchester University Press, 2013), p. 14.

[53]   *tephen White, Communism and its Collapse (Routledge, 2002), p. 22.*